A YEAR WITH THE WIND

A YEAR
WITH THE
WIND

Hanna Konola

GIBBS SMITH
TO ENRICH AND INSPIRE HUMANKIND

In April, I gently fly kites in the sky.

In May, I blow
flower petals here and there.

In June, I push
soft summer clouds in the sky.

In July, I blow
boats on their way!

In August, I bring rain clouds
from the faraway seas.

In September, I let birds
ride on my back toward the south.

In October, I twist and twirl
and strip leaves off the trees!

In November, I blow
leaves into big piles with mighty gusts.

In December, I dance around with snowflakes.

In January,
I blow some speed
for skaters on ice!

In February, I sometimes
stay very still.

In March, I tickle your cheeks
and look forward to a new spring!

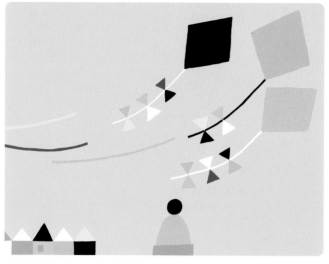

April

May

August

September

December

January

June

July

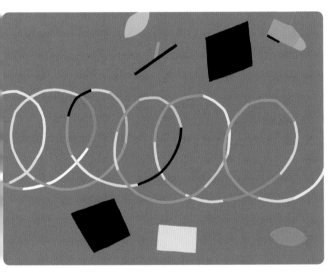

October

November

February

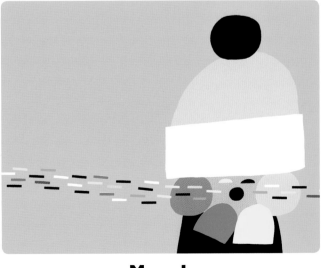

March

First published in Finland
Original title: *Tuulen vuosi* Copyright © by Hanna Konola and
Etana Editions 2016
Text and Illustrations © 2016 Hanna Konola and Etana Editions
Graphic Design © 2016 Etana Editions

Published in the United States of America by
Gibbs Smith
P.O. Box 667
Layton, Utah 84041
1.800.835.4993 orders
www.gibbs-smith.com

Published in agreement with Koja Agency
Text and Illustrations © 2018 Hanna Konola and Etana Editions
Graphic design by Etana Editions

Manufactured in January 2018 in Hong Kong by Toppan
Printing Co.

First Edition
22 21 20 19 18   5 4 3 2 1

Printed and bound in Hong Kong
Gibbs Smith books are printed on either recycled, 100% post-
consumer waste, FSC-certified papers or on paper produced
from sustainable PEFC-certified forest/controlled wood source.
Learn more at www.pefc.org.

Library of Congress Control Number: 2017950588
ISBN: 978-1-4236-4925-0